Be Bold,
DOMINATE
and Succeed In
Marketing
For Today's Digital World
On A Limited Budget

Wayne Elsey

WEE Publishing

ORLANDO

Published by WEE Publishing

520 N. Semoran Blvd., Suite 200, Orlando, FL 32807

ISBN: 978-0-578-16782-4

Dedication

To my schoolteacher, Mr.****, who told me I was an idiot and would not amount to anything. And, to my teacher MS Busch who said, "YOU matter, YOU can do anything and don't let stupid people get you down."

TABLE OF CONTENTS

Recently I published Not Your Father's Charity: The Rise And Fail Of Charities And What You Can Do To Be Ready. That book sounded the alarm to nonprofits about the changes happening in the social sector. The primary reason for this is, of course, technology and the digital revolution.

That book was for those, "…who are looking to provide a cure, in addition to the Band-Aid." It talked about the difference between philanthropy and charity and how organizations need to have bold ideas and vision to meet the challenges of today head-on. The book also highlighted nonprofits and people who were making a greater difference in the world. As someone who was the founder of a nonprofit that went from zero to over $70 million in revenue in less than five years and who established a successful social enterprise, Funds2Orgs, I wanted to give strategies and thoughts on how to "go big" organizationally or with vision.

However, I know the majority of nonprofits operate with a budget of less than $1 million. So, this time around, this book is written with these social sector entities in mind. Perhaps, you work for one of these organizations. I've come across countless small and medium-sized nonprofits and even for-profit social enterprises that were looking to succeed. They typically have a great cause, a good idea and a lot of passion.

But you know something? Sometimes it's tough to sing and dance at the same time.

As I mentioned, I have a social enterprise, but I also have a number of other portfolio brands under Wayne Elsey Enterprises. I've been in the business world for 35 years. I know one of the key ingredients to success is marketing with a 21st Century understanding. That's why my other companies focus on marketing–including digital marketing, branding and strategy, among other things. My companies and the team that works with me couldn't be successful if we weren't focused on marketing every day.

As I was writing my earlier book, I kept on thinking of those small and medium-sized mom and pop organizations all over the United States and the world. Each and every day, 24/7/365, leaders and staff for organizations work tirelessly. Many of them have small budgets and are doing incredible work with limited means. Others may have larger budgets, but most of the money is in their program costs. Their operational costs—including marketing—are on a shoestring.

Every business day, I get the opportunity to speak to someone in one of these nonprofits or social enterprises. More often than not, when I ask someone why he or she does the work, they tell me a very personal story that resonates with them. I've included some in this book, but typically I change his or her name and identifying information to safeguard privacy.

I know many cancer survivors, for instance, who went down a different path once they were diagnosed with cancer. They worked in some major national or international company somewhere when they received the diagnosis. Then they fought this dreaded disease. And, when they conquered it, he or she decided to spend the rest of their lives helping others do the same thing.

I know survivors of domestic violence who suffered terrible abuse at the hands of a spouse or partner who was supposed to love and care for them. Instead, the domestic abuse survivors found themselves on the receiving end of punches, slaps and kicks. When they managed to find the strength and resources to help them out of this life-threatening situation, they went on to commit their lives to helping others get out of similar circumstances.

I know pastors, who have been called by God to minister to the poor, infirm, children and families in their local communities. These pastors started their careers in ministry working tirelessly within a church under the guidance of an experienced priest or reverend. And then, the time came that they too have been called to lead their own congregation.

I know these people, as I'm sure you do, who are doing good—even great—work trying to make our planet and all the creatures that live on it better. Millions of people around the world, and right here at home, start nonprofits and social enterprises every year. Then, they're faced with not only delivering excellent quality programs, but also dealing with the daily issues of money, marketing and raising awareness.

This book is for those leaders, volunteers, staff members and others who care about the social sector. It doesn't matter if you're involved in a nonprofit or a for-profit social enterprise. Perhaps the organization you care about is less than a year old. Or, maybe that organization is decades old but has struggled to rebrand itself for today's younger generations and more diverse donors.

Whatever the case, my intention is to write a book that helps those small and medium-sized organizations, who want to learn about digital marketing, including social media. But, more importantly, I want to offer strategies, ideas and tips you can use now–particularly if you don't have a large budget.

There are things you can do, even with limited means, to market and promote your organization. The fact that you're reading this book in the 21st Century is a distinct advantage. There are tools and technologies today that were simply not available five, ten and fifteen years ago. It may take a little time and some effort, but if you're committed to figuring out how to get the word out about your organization, hopefully, this book will help you.

ONE

Build It And They Don't Come

"The best way to predict the future is to create it." – Peter Drucker

Recently, I read about a survey that stated that 60 percent of nonprofits do not have a website or a Facebook page. Frankly, I was surprised by this statistic. I thought that once anyone decides to set up a nonprofit or social enterprise, one of the first things they do is claim their space on the Internet. Since I work with social sector organizations, this made it abundantly clear that my next book would be about digital marketing and how to succeed in today's world.

I then thought about the "old days". If you're of a certain age, you remember when the Internet started to creep into the work environment. Inevitably, we all got to a point when any business or organization that wanted to market themselves had to develop a website. In those days it was an expensive, but a necessary proposition, typically costing thousands of dollars.

But then, perhaps you were like me and understood that simply building a website was not going to do much except set up a presence on the Internet. It wouldn't do any good if no one knew where to find you on the Internet. To have that website work for you, you had to promote actively and market it. I remember during those early days that there were plenty of organizations with leaders demanding websites be created, only to ask themselves, "Now what?"

As I prepared for this book and began making mental notes on marketing before starting to write, I thought of situations. I had come across organizations that had the best of intentions, but they were missing the boat on marketing.

Even today, I've spoken to plenty of leaders who make a substantial investment (when they don't have to) into a website. Then they wonder why people aren't finding them, donating or otherwise getting engaged with their cause.

Not too long ago, I was on the telephone with a wonderful nonprofit leader. Miriam has a small school in the middle of the country. She is a passionate educator who cares very much for the futures of all her students. Her school is relatively new–less than five years old. She has a dedicated administrative staff and teachers who give it their best each day.

The Website

With a new school came expenses. While the government does help fund the school, each day Miriam has to make decisions, as do her teachers, about how they spend money. If you have a child attending school, you've probably experienced a lot of fundraisers and have donated supplies. Schools have cut arts and sports programs. Parents pitch in to help the classroom teacher pay for a local trip to the museum or zoo because the school can't fund it.

On a recent day when Miriam and I spoke, she was telling me that she wanted to upgrade the school's website. The site did not have functionality to accept donations. She wondered if she made it user-friendly, if they would have more people support her inner-city school.

When I asked Miriam how much designers and web developers were telling her that it would cost to update and upgrade her site, she told me something close to $5,000.

"Whoa, $5,000?" I repeated, "You don't need to spend anywhere close to that today. Question for you, Miriam, do you have a marketing plan or a way to reach out so you can create relationships with prospective supporters to the school?"

Miriam said, "No", rather flatly.

"Don't worry. You've been so good with us, my team will work with you and we'll get something together to update your website. We'll also help you with ideas on how to get people to find you and support you for those kids you're teaching," I said, "And, it's not going to cost anywhere near $5,000."

Churches, nonprofits, schools or social enterprises that are just starting out or have limited means can still have a compelling site that does not have to break the bank. Additionally, there are concrete steps and strategies that small organizations can do to promote themselves and gain more supporters. The trick is to develop a presence, never stop providing added value and understand the tools you have at your disposal.

As I mentioned in my introduction, this book is targeted to the countless organizations that operate with a budget under $1 million. Limited resources hamper their ability to promote themselves. It's also meant for churches, schools and nonprofits that may have larger budgets, but work with small general operating budgets. I'm going to tell you how to organically grow your lists and promote your organization. I'm also going to give you strategies and ideas on how to do this effectively.

What Is Marketing?

So, let's start with what the concept of "marketing" really is in the business world. I've seen through the years people use this word generically, but may not always know what it means. I think it's important to start here, and then we'll build together as you progress through the book. We need to build the foundation first for the more in-depth knowledge and techniques to make sense.

Very simply, marketing is the process of informing your constituents and prospective supporters why they should support your efforts over those of your competitor. Everything you do in marketing, even if it does not seem so, is geared toward influencing your target audience. You want them to view you as the expert in your field, which you are! You give them this understanding by giving them relevant and pertinent information and value. You want them to view your products and services, or in the case of a social sector organization, your mission and programs as excellent in quality and worthy of support.

I'm not going to go too deep into marketing theory, but in a moment, I will mention the classic four Ps of marketing (I have an additional P). I think they help organizations formulate questions they should answer for effective marketing. We know that we live, work, learn and operate in a very different world. The digital revolution we're experiencing is forcing everyone to embrace technology.

I think it's important to recognize that the digital revolution has caused marketers to continue to develop their thinking around marketing. Some professional marketers have expanded upon them and say there are more Ps to add to the mix, such as process and physical environment. Still others, like Kimberly Kadlec, the former Worldwide Vice President, Global Marketing Group at Johnson and Johnson coined the four new Ps: purpose, presence, proximity and partnerships.

However, I think for our purposes and the book, we can stay with the classic four Ps as our focus, with an additional one. There are elements of the traditional Ps that nonprofits and social enterprises, particularly the smaller ones, need to discuss and define to have a chance of being successful in marketing.

Digital Marketing and Content Marketing

It's important to understand content and digital marketing because you're probably hearing a lot about it these days. I could write a number of books on every aspect of marketing. But, I want to make sure this book is easy and simple for those who are reading it as a resource. That said, I do want to at least draw your attention to content and digital marketing because they are important. You'll see those terms thread through in this book.

Think of content marketing as the value you are providing your supporters and followers. It's the thought leadership that you offer in given areas. Content marketing helps inform your donors, and it educates those who follow you. Content marketing can be serious or entertaining. It includes the content that you're distributing to your constituents, the experience it provides and the metrics.

Digital marketing is simply marketing that is accomplished using digital technology. This can mean emails, electronic newsletters, blogs, podcasts, ebooks, digital white papers, your website, social media, being mobile, etc. Think of everything you do to promote and inform your supporters about your organization digitally and that's digital marketing. More broadly speaking, it also includes the analysis and data gathered to measure success or gain insights.

The Five Ps of Marketing

If you remember the four Ps, they'll help you go a long way toward being effective in your marketing efforts. The classic four Ps of marketing are as follows: product, promotion, price and place.

So what do they mean?

Product = the solution to the need

Promotion = the information you offer

Price = the value you place on the solution

Place = how you're distributing your product or service

I believe there is one more: P = People, which means that organizations should recognize that their customers or donors have power. People have more to do and say about our brands than ever before. They have power. They can speak about your brand or organization at the grocery store or use their platforms on social media. It's important for organizations to recognize that supporters should be considered brand ambassadors.

How can we apply the Ps to the social sector? What do they mean for any nonprofit or social enterprise?

Let's break it all down and discuss some of the questions your organization should be asking now if it hasn't already.

Product
- How is your organization branded? In other words, beyond your organization's name, when a donor or supporter hears your name or sees your logo, what do they think? What images does it invoke in them?
- How do you differentiate yourself from your competitors? We know there are likely others doing what you do. What makes your organization unique and different from anyone else addressing a similar issue?
- What do your donors want to see in the implementation of your mission that will move him or her to want to support your organization? So, for instance, what metrics and results do donors want to see? What impact is your organization making in society?
- Within, that framework, what need does it satisfy within the do-

nor? Remember, individual donors will tend to support your organization because it provides a certain emotional satisfaction. Perhaps they're cancer survivors who support your charity addressing the eradication of the disease. Maybe they're parents who believe in an excellent quality of education for all children. Or, they might be professionals who believe in a highly educated workforce.

- How can your donors experience your work? How can they engage with it? We know that it's important to get people involved in the cause. The best way is to allow donors and prospective supporters to see your work in action.

Place

- Where can those who need your service find you? Also, where can donors and others who are looking to support an organization such as yours find you? How about others who want to partner with you; how do they find you? Do you have an office? Social media? Do you collaborate with local partners who refer you?
- Do you have community engagement staff?
- If you engage with your local community, how do you accomplish this? Do you have events? Do your staff members attend local conferences or trade association meetings?

Price

- What is the per capita cost to deliver your programs?
- What are your program costs?
- What are your operating costs?
- For donors and supporters, if they become involved, do you have a giving or membership levels?
- If so, what are the benefits of being a supporter?
- What amount qualifies someone as a major donor?
- Do you ask your donors to become sustaining donors on a monthly, bi-monthly or quarterly basis by contributing a certain dollar amount?
- What do you do around donations as compared to other social sector organizations in your neighborhood, particularly those who are doing similar work to you?

Promotion

- Where do you market to those in need of your services? For example, do local partners refer you?

- Where do you promote to supporters and donors? Do you reach out and market to them on your website, through a blog, advertising, media, direct response, social media, etc.?
- How often do you market to those who need your services?
- How often do you promote to prospects and your current donors and supporters?
- Do you have targeted campaigns that take advantage of, for instance, the holiday season when most people give to charity?
- Do you know how your competitors market their organization and when? How does your organization compare?

People

- How is your organization engaging with its supporters?
- How are you getting your donors involved with your brand?
- What tools have you provided your champions to help you promote your brand?
- What messages do you give your donors and activists to share with their circles of influence?
- How do you measure supporter involvement with your organization?
- How do you show your champions–on a regular basis–that you value their support?

If you're a leader in the social sector, take some time to sit with your team to discuss the five Ps. Ask your team members to help you answer these questions. If you're a start-up, take the time from the beginning to do it right. And, if you've been around for a while, but want to jump-start your marketing, take a couple of hours with your staff to go through the five Ps.

If you have others questions around product, price, promotion, place and people–ask them. Don't forget, your nonprofit or social enterprise has to be a living and breathing entity. You want to make sure that you're as effective as possible in marketing, so you have the greatest amount of impact as it relates to your mission.

With the advent of the Internet and digital marketing, you probably see a ton of stuff about how to do this or that. Everyone has a solution for your troubles. How do you make sense of it all and how do you know what advice to take and what to toss?

Begin by reminding yourself that you don't have to do everything! It's impossible. Not every strategy and tip even in this book will work for your organization. Pick and choose ideas and ways of doing things that will make sense for you and will complement your overall efforts. Second, if you need help–get it.

Marketing is hard work, and it takes a lot of time and staff resources. If you need to find a social media volunteer, for example, find one. If you need to find someone to help you manage your overall marketing, but you don't have the money, there are still other things you can do. Once you've made the decision to amp up your content and digital marketing efforts, get a point person to be accountable and responsible for helping you. We'll talk more about how to find help in the next chapter.

TWO

How Can I Find Help?

"Good marketers see consumers as complete human beings with all the dimensions real people have." – Jonah Sachs

I know you have a lot to do. I've been there. Working at a nonprofit or social enterprise is very hard work. You need to keep a million balls in the air–all while hopping on one foot. Did I mention you also had to have one hand behind your back?

When people start a nonprofit, school, church or social enterprise, they typically want to see change happen. They start out with an idea, and they are so focused on it that, hopefully, they'll be able to recruit supporters to join them.

Founders, leaders and others create great programs to serve their communities through their organization. They set out to raise money for those programs. They may ask volunteers or staff to help them with fundraising. But, a critical step toward this goal for any program is marketing.

Not too long ago, I had a conversation with a very passionate pastor of a small church in Florida. He arrived from his native country of Kenya less than five years ago. From his little church, he ministers to an immigrant community. For the purposes of this book, I will call him Fr. Elea.

Fr. Elea and His New Nonprofit
Fr. Elea loves this nation, but he also loves the country where he grew up.

During our conversation, he told me about the systemic need for Kenya to do better at educating children in his country. He also expressed his concern for educating young girls who tend to have more challenges, for societal reasons, in receiving an education.

Fr. Elea is a small man in stature, but he is big on vision. "I want to start a school. But it may take me some time to raise money for a school. So, in the meantime, I want to work with established schools and make them better," he told me and continued, "I want to get as many children educated as I possibly can."

"How do you plan on doing that?" I asked.

"I already have a group of volunteers here at the church who want to help me. We're in the process of establishing a nonprofit," he said proudly with a wide grin.

"That's great!"

"Yes, and we're looking to raise money."

"Wonderful, it sounds like your parishioners will help you."

"Yes, I think so."

"Do you have people who can help you raise awareness about what you plan to do so it'll be easier to raise money?"

"I'm working on that," he told me, "I have very smart people in business who want to help."

"Do you have anyone who is helping you on the day-to-day since you're busy with the new nonprofit and here at your church with your congregation?"

"No, it's just me. I will take care of all the administration."

"With all due respect, Fr. Elea, you may need a little more help."

And, then we set off discussing ideas for recruiting other supportive people besides busy potential board members. Board leaders only have a few hours to spare each month for his new nonprofit.

To support your programs, you need money. To get donors to invest in your organization, you need for them to know about you. I promised you I would give you concrete strategies and tips you can use to get your name out there and raise awareness. Unless you have some money to pay someone as your marketing manager, you're going to need some extra hands. So here goes.

If you're at an organization that does not have the financial resources to get someone to help you market there are places you can look for that extra help at low or no cost. Some of the following options may not have individuals who have direct nonprofit or social enterprise experience. However, they may have marketing experience, even if it's in a for-profit setting. Other resources will connect you with professionals in the social sector who are willing to lend their time and marketing expertise to your organization.

VOLUNTEERMATCH.ORG

VolunteerMatch has a database of over 100,000 nonprofits around the world. They spotlight groups and help connect volunteers with organizations, both locally and virtually.

As of this writing, VolunteerMatch has 93,585 Active Opportunities at 100,364 organizations around the world and has made over 9.2 million referrals for volunteering since 1998.

SCORE

The Small Business Administration established SCORE as "a nonprofit association dedicated to helping small businesses get off the ground, grow and meet their goals through education and mentorship." With a cadre of over 11,000 volunteers throughout the United States, SCORE works with small businesses, including nonprofits, in need of advice and counsel. Because of their volunteer network, they are typically able to offer their services at no charge or a low fee.

Specifically as it relates to marketing, they can offer advice, mentoring and have resources for topics such as advertising, branding, engagement, online marketing and social media.

MicroMentor

MicroMentor is a free social network that matches entrepreneurs and volunteer business mentors. This platform has been featured on The New York Times, The Wall Street Journal and Forbes. Once you sign up with MicroMentor, you set your goals and volunteer schedule. You decide how you will meet with your mentor and how often to achieve your goals.

Taproot Foundation

The Taproot Foundation provides pro-bono service grants to nonprofit organizations. This is an excellent organization with nonprofit professionals volunteering their time and expertise. As of this writing, they have provided over $146 million in volunteer time. Taproot began operating out of New York City, but they've expanded their services to include the following cities: Chicago, Los Angeles, San Francisco and Washington D.C.

With a service grant, organizations that are accepted will be assigned a team to work with them of 5 to 6 professionals. These experts will deliver services valued at $45,000 or more at no cost to the nonprofit. Taproot focuses on in the following areas: marketing, design, technology, management and strategic planning.

If you happen to have your 501(c)(3) in one of the previously mentioned cities, check out their service grant criteria before applying. They are very specific concerning organizations they help.

Catchafire

Cathafire is a straightforward site, which helps organizations looking for volunteers with professionals who can assist in marketing. They also have other areas, including fundraising and operations. Simply list the project you need to get done. For instance, you can include creating a website, social media planning, graphic design and other marketing efforts. You can browse through a list of volunteer professionals who can help you execute. When you find someone who is of interest, or they find you, you can schedule a consultation and take it from there.

Your Local University

A colleague I know has found that working with a graduate student from a local university has typically provided him with a good extra pair of hands. It's important to note that schools have started to crack down on unpaid internships because of abuses of "free labor", among other things. So, do as my associate does and pay a stipend to graduate students who are obtaining degrees in nonprofit or social enterprise studies. In exchange for a paid internship, you may find a young professional who can put together a marketing or social media plan for you and perhaps even execute it. Additionally, he or she may help you develop and start an outreach effort.

Ideally, my colleague has told me the most fruitful paid internships have been when the student integrates the work he or she is doing into their university course of study. In other words, when the student has used your organization and the work done for a particular project in their class or as a case study. In those instances, my associate has found the work to be of a high caliber. Both he and the intern have felt they have been on the good end of a win/win collaboration.

Now that you have various sources for finding volunteer help, you should feel confident. You should find someone to work with who is aligned with your mission and wants to see you succeed.

There's one last note. Before looking for a volunteer, make sure to think through the following. This will help you have a rewarding and mutually beneficial relationship with your volunteer:

- Write a position description for your volunteer. This will help you have clear thinking of what you would like your volunteer to do. It will also give your volunteer an understanding about your goals and expectations. Make sure the description notes the number of hours involved for your volunteer per week. More than likely your volunteer, especially a professional, will only be able to help fewer than 8 hours per week. An option is to create opportunities for a high-level volunteer who creates the strategy. And, you can have a junior volunteer who handles most of the implementation. Also, make sure you define the requisite skills that your volunteer(s) must possess.

- Make sure when you are recruiting for a volunteer that you're clear with your messaging. You want to "sell" your organization. Give the benefits of volunteering for your nonprofit or social enterprise and relay the responsibilities required for the role.

- Promote your volunteer opportunity on your website and any social media platforms you may be using. Additionally, send out information in any newsletter or collateral material that you may be sending to your constituents. Remember, your supporters are the best place to start and help you promote your volunteer opportunity.

- When you're recruiting a volunteer for marketing, treat it as a professional recruitment opportunity. Out of the inquiries you receive, take the time to interview candidates in person. Check references. Make sure they're aligned to your mission and goals and have the skill sets you need to take kick-start your marketing. Once you've selected a candidate, get him or her on board as soon as possible to keep momentum. And, make it a point to inform other volunteer candidates that you have chosen someone else who is more aligned to your criteria.

THREE

How Do We Write A Marketing Plan?

"I've learned that people will forget what you said, people will forget what you did, but people will never forget how you made them feel." – Maya Angelou

Helping Inner-City Students
Ignacio started a small nonprofit in the Southeast.

It's a wonderful organization. They are a startup charity focused on getting youth in under-served inner-city neighborhoods into college. They do this by providing supplemental education to what the public schools offer the kids. After the school day, middle and high school students show up at this nonprofit for more academic support and enrichment programs.

Ignacio and his team are focused on making sure as many inner-city students graduate high school and go on to college. In this particular city, public high school graduation rates are below 60 percent. Most of the kids in the neighborhoods where he works are lucky to get a high school diploma, and it's an incredible feat to have young adults graduate college. Ignacio has partnered with other youth enrichment programs and the local schools to change the life path of the students his organization serves.

During the course of my work, I met a man dedicated to the lives of the kids in his neighborhood. Ignacio, who goes by the nickname "Iggy", is the son of an American mother and a Mexican father. Although Iggy was born in the United States, his parents soon moved back to Mexico City to raise their family. He lived there for many years until he became an adult and was transferred by an international company to the States to work in finance.

In early 2000, Iggy was living in Manhattan. He loved what he was doing, the money he was making and the energy of New York. Things couldn't be better at the beginning of the new century.

But then 9/11 happened.

Like many people who lived in New York at the time, life changed forever that day. Even though a new normal settled in, those who were present have the images and events of September 11th burned in their collective memory.

At the time, Iggy had done some volunteer work on a board at a charter school, and he became familiar with the issues facing inner-city youth in the city. Once the immediate rawness of 9/11 passed, Iggy decided to quit his high-paying job, move to a city in the U.S. closer to his family in Mexico and start a nonprofit organization. He knew that inner-city students across the country were struggling. He was determined to change it.

After my talk with his group, Iggy and I spent some time talking over dinner. Iggy is a slender man who runs marathons and is physically fit. He speaks English with an accent having lived his youth and even some of his early adult years in Mexico. His mother started a cross-border nonprofit and Iggy was raised to help always those who were not as fortunate as he was in life.

Like all startups, Iggy's organization is doing everything at the same time. One of the topics Iggy and I spoke about was marketing. Nonprofits, especially those without name brand recognition, need to focus a lot of time and effort to get their name out into the community.

What's a Marketing Plan?

Let's start with the basics. A marketing plan is simply a road map. Startups are sometimes tempted to just "do everything" and see what sticks. Sometimes this scattershot approach can have some success in an area or two. But, overall, it's a lot of energy that is better spent taking the time to understand where you are and where you want to go.

Your marketing plan will help you build awareness for your organization with your target audience. More than likely, "everyone" in your community is not a potential supporter. Your marketing plan will help you define who to approach, so you're able to reach out to the prospective supporters most likely to be interested in your mission.

With your marketing plan, you'll have the path to building an audience that's most likely to want to become involved with your organization. It'll also help you build brand loyalty because your marketing plan will include strategies for actively engaging with your supporters.

Remember Your 5 Ps

When you're in the process of developing a marketing plan, you'll want to look and refer to your 5 Ps. Use them as a guide and resource to help inform your decisions around you marketing efforts. They're critical building blocks in developing your plan. If you find it beneficial, join these elements within the body of your marketing roadmap.

Product = the solution to the need

Promotion = the information you offer

Price = the value you place on the solution

Place = how you're distributing your product or service

People = your donors and supporters

Elements of a Simple Marketing Plan

If you do some research, you'll find some variations on developing a marketing plan. That's okay. For the purposes of this book, I'll lay out key points that you should make sure your marketing plan includes, at a minimum.

Brand

Very simply, your brand is everything that your supporters think and feel when they hear your name. I bet as you read the following brand names, they conjure up images in your mind: Apple, Nike, Save the Children or the Salvation Army.

When you think of these brands, it's highly likely that you see colors, logos, images and these prompt some emotional connection for you.

Brand Promise, Positioning and Messaging

A brand promise is incorporated in all of your nonprofit's marketing and promotional activities, including your digital marketing. By communicating through visuals (colors and your logo, for instance), consistent words and messages, you're creating an image in the minds of your supporters. Your brand promise inspires your champions to engage with you intellectually and emotionally.

Your brand position helps differentiate your brand from that of your competitors. For example, if I write, "Coke" and then "Pepsi", you'll formulate different images for each brand in your mind. You'll see different colors and logos. You may think of different tastes. You may think you prefer one over the other if you drink carbonated soda. That's brand positioning.

Messaging is the right language that you use to communicate to your supporters and the public about your brand.

Target Market

When you're thinking of potential supporters, the first question you need to ask yourself is who they would be. Who do you want to target? Again, you don't want to go after everyone and anyone with a pulse. That's a tough way to approach building your brand. So, take the time as you begin to develop your marketing plan to think about who would likely support your organization.

If you work at an organization with a mission to support families who are dealing with cancer, you're probably looking for different supporters than if you're working at a soup kitchen. You want to understand your target audience. This will help you find the right groups, websites, print and digital media, etc. where you might want to spend any advertising dollars. It'll also help you be clear about any editors you may want to approach for public relations stories.

Organizational and Marketing Goals

Your marketing plan should be aligned with your organizational goals and objectives. In developing your marketing plan for the upcoming year, be clear about your charity's goals. Will you be starting a new program?

Will you be undertaking a capital campaign? Will you be expanding in revenue or staff size?

By having a clear understanding of your organizational goals, you'll help your marketing people know where to focus. If you're starting a new program, for instance, your marketing team will understand that they have to prepare for some rollout.

Once your marketing pros understand what is done organizationally, they can formulate marketing goals in support of your overall efforts.

Programs

When you're clear about your target audience and organizational goals, you want to have a good understanding of your nonprofit or social enterprise programs. The reason for this is to carry out two objectives:

1) If you work at a charity focused on supporting cancer patients, you want to reach families who are dealing with the disease. Remember, individuals who have some connection or history with your mission will become your best supporters; and,

2) You want to explain in easy to understand language the excellent programs you deliver in your community. Your supporters will want to know what you're doing and how you're doing it, as well as the results. This is a driver to getting them engaged with your organization.

Competition

I've said several times; many for-profit and non-profit start-ups do not understand their competition. This is a mistake. You need to know who's out there doing something similar to you. You also need to explain what makes you different (and better) than your competition.

If your organization is a church or school, for instance, are there others in your neighborhood seeking to recruit the same students and supporters? If the nonprofit is an arts program, are there others doing the same thing? And, always, what makes your brand different from your competitors? What is your organization's unique value proposition? What are you offering the people your serve? How do you treat and engage with your supporters?

Marketing Strategies and Tactics

As you continue to develop your marketing plan, you want to develop the strategies that will support your goals. How do you intend to market your organization, its programs and initiatives? In the strategies below, you'll want to outline specific tactics that you'll use to execute each strategy.

Marketing strategies for you to consider in the promotion of your brand should include the following:

- Website: How will you make sure you create a mobile-friendly website with ongoing search engine optimization (SEO) and search engine marketing (SEM)?

- Networking: Will you be going to events such as professional groups, conferences, seminars, association events or your local business chamber of commerce meetings to network with individuals who may become supporters?

- Direct Response: Will your social enterprise be looking to create a direct mail or email campaigns? Will there be telephone outreach?

- Social Media: What social media platforms should you use to focus your efforts? My suggestion is to be represented at least on Facebook and Twitter. More on that later. There are countless social media platforms. Learn about them and decide which appeal to you and which your supporters likely use.

- Advertising: If you choose to advertise your nonprofit or social enterprise, decide what publications would make sense. Remember where your target audience is likely to be found.

- Public Relations: Whereas advertising is paid promotion, public relations is unpaid. Consider print and digital editors to reach out to and pitch stories about your organization. Think about developing press releases as you announce new programs, events or initiatives.

- Blogging: Your donors want to hear from you in different ways. Blogging is a great way to communicate with supporters, keep yourself top of mind and offer them a value add.

- Expert: Your CEO or executive director is an expert within your community. When there is news that is relevant to the work you're doing, think about having your CEO pitched to various sources. You can reach out to television, digital, print and radio sources to give his or her thinking on the issues.

Budget

Things always come down to money. Think about how much you can afford. If you have a volunteer developing and executing your marketing plan that's great. But remember, you'll probably have to pay something for a website, to attend events, or use some digital tools that may help make that strategy more efficient. Think carefully about your dollars and cents, but don't be penny-wise and pound-foolish.

Results

Finally, develop ways that you'll be able to test approaches and analyze results for your marketing. If down the line you see one effort that's working and a couple that are not, you'll want to make adjustments. But to make those changes, you'll have to know what works and what doesn't.

FOUR

Creating An Effective Website

"Instead of using technology to automate processes, think about using technology to enhance human interaction." – Tony Zambito

I mentioned earlier in the book that I recently read that as many as 60 percent of nonprofit organizations do not have a website. That's a problem.

Think about it. How are people supposed to find those organizations? Let's assume that many or most of these charities have a brick and mortar office somewhere in their community. That's great, but it's not enough. Perhaps people will stumble upon your office and decide to walk in and see what it's all about, but that's not likely.

For those organizations that do not have a website, this is a situation where they're thinking they are saving money but are losing it. A website is just as important as a physical office, although, in today's world, many businesses work remotely.

Online giving continues to grow. In 2013, the Chronicle of Philanthropy published a study that found online giving accounted for $2.1 billion in donations, which was an increase of 14 percent over 2011. And, according to Nonprofit Hub, 60 percent of donors will check out your site as they consider making a donation. Quite simply, if you don't have a website, you're limiting yourself to donors and supporters who are only in your neighborhood and may have heard of your nonprofit somehow.

And, what of those organizations that do have a website? That's a great start, but if your website is not mobile (I know I keep saying that), user-friendly and easy to navigate, it's not as effective as you think.

My Website Research

During the course of writing this book, I did a little research of my own and I went on nonprofit, school, church and social enterprise websites to see how organizations were presenting themselves on the Internet. Of course, this is not scientific in any way, but it didn't take me long to compile a list of issues that I view as challenges to a having an engaging site.

Following are some of the things I found:

- Text heavy and minimal pictures.
- Low-quality graphics and images.
- Too much content and too small font sizes.
- Content that was too academic, and frankly, boring.
- Content that was three and four years old. Really–nothing new has happened?
- Not mobile friendly.
- No donation page and if there was a donation page, it was not easy to navigate to it from any place on the website.
- No pictures or stories of individuals and families being served.
- No pictures or stories of donors or volunteers so people can "see" themselves in those positions.
- No social media following or sharing so supporters can easily communicate what you're about to others.
- Link rot! In other words, broken links that don't work properly.

Those are simply some of the issues that I found on multiple websites, and it didn't take me long to find these examples.

I'm a big believer that right out of the box, you're always out to make a great first impression! It doesn't matter how much money you spent or didn't spend. You need to communicate to the public and your constituents that you're successful and present yourself in an excellent way.

Why?

Because it will help them trust you!

Let me ask you something. Would you trust an organization, let alone support it if everything they presented looked as if an amateur did it? Would you think they're doing the best they can toward their mission? Would you think they are good stewards of your donations and support? Just because you don't have a lot of money doesn't mean you can't take the time to be an expert and show excellence.

Getting Started on Your Website

So, let's get started. If you don't have a website or are looking to update an existing site that is old and tired, it's time to make a change.

Remember from the outset, you're looking to create a mobile-ready, visually appealing and easy to navigate site. It will represent the excellent work you do. In other words, you want a website using responsive web design.

Responsive web design provides a mobile-ready and user-friendly website experience. This means that if an end-user is viewing your site on his or her desktop, when he or she switches devices to check it out on a mobile it will be responsive. By that, I mean that its responsive design focuses on key elements of the user experience. The pages of your site, for instance, will look great whether someone is viewing it on a computer, tablet or mobile.

Nature Conservancy and Heifer International

Two sites that I would recommend you take a look at for excellent responsive web design are Heifer and Nature Conservancy. Take a moment and have your desktop as well as another device such as a tablet or a mobile readily available. I want to highlight a few reasons why these two sites are exceptional websites.

Let's begin with Nature Conservancy. If you check its website, you're going to see a very beautiful site. Its got appealing colors and you'll see how incredibly easy it is to navigate. Notice that the font size is large so people can easily read it. If you scroll across the navigation bar across the top, you'll find drop down menus that help you go wherever you're interested in going on the site.

Notice the "Donate Now" button on the upper-right of the website. If you navigate away from the home page, you will always have the "Donate Now" button in view. That's important.

On their homepage, they have a carousel of pictures, which ensures the page is not static and boring. At present as I write this book, one of these pictures has a call to action asking people to enter their photo contest.

As you scroll down, you'll see more buttons and links that can take you to other places on the website if you're interested. And, about midway down the home page, they're providing you with the quantifiable facts with graphics about the work they do. With those facts, you see another call to action asking you to "Join Us".

Scroll down to the bottom third of the homepage, and you'll see news. You'll also see how you can stay connected with them on Facebook, Twitter, Instagram, etc. You'll see a widget where you can join their database and receive their newsletter. At the bottom, you'll see the footer where you have a "map" with corresponding links to pages.

Now, pick up your mobile or tablet and go to the Nature Conservancy site. I'm doing it on my cell phone as I write. Out of the gate, you see the carousel you saw on the desktop. You see the same color palette. Keep on scrolling down and you'll see the same elements we just went through, including social media buttons and the newsletter widget.

With respect to the "Donate Now" button on the mobile version of the site, you'll find it at the top. Mobile is about easy navigation and social media. Notice on your mobile how the Facebook, Twitter and email buttons are static at the bottom of your device screen. This is another call to action to follow the organization using social media, or perhaps email the site to a friend!

Now let's take a quick look at Heifer International. Again, let's begin on your desktop. Just as you saw on the Nature Conservancy's page, you will find easy to navigate (and readable) links with drop-down menus for more information on this site as well. The colors are appealing and easy on the eyes. If you scroll down a little further, you'll currently see a video play button to engage you in their story. And below that, you have another donation button.

Notice the large pictures and visuals. Both sites use pictures effectively to communicate. They are not text heavy and cumbersome. No one's got time to read dense text. The fact is someone will stay on your website for only a few seconds unless you engage them. And, a picture is still very much worth a thousand words!

If you continue to scroll down the site, you'll see graphics and quantified facts to grab your attention. Heifer does the donation button differently. While the Nature Conservancy had it as a static button at the top of the website, so you always had it present wherever you went on the site, Heifer does not do that. Instead, the organization has chosen to communicate their story throughout and then keep on providing you with calls to action for financial support with buttons placed as you scroll.

That being said, Heifer is known for its "Gift Catalog". In reality, this is another and ingenious way to give to the organization. If you navigate around the site, the "Gift Catalog" is always present.

I have a friend who "has everything" and her friends "have everything" too. She has given these social good "gifts" from Heifer for a birthday, holiday, graduation, anniversary gifts, etc. for years. Essentially, she selects a gift from Heifer and donates in the name of someone she knows. However, a "gift" can also be considered a donation gift to Heifer from you to the organization.

I will tell you that, frankly, if I were developing a nonprofit website, I would have a static donation button, so it's present anywhere you went on the site. However, if you develop a site as engaging as Heifer's, or perhaps you have a "gift catalog" as well, you can test out the strategy of having many opportunities (and buttons) to donate.

Now let's take a moment and look at the same site on a mobile or tablet device. Again, as I write this, I'm checking it out on my cell phone.

When you view the Heifer site on a mobile, you'll see–just like the Nature Conservancy–that you have a call to action to either join their mailing list or donate. The colors are the same as you saw on the desktop. Scroll a little and you'll see the video inviting you to view it. And, as you keep scrolling down the page, you'll see the same elements that were found on the desktop version on the mobile site as well. They have multiple buttons for donations, and you'll see their social media calls to action.

Folks, these two organizations are examples of nonprofits that have done excellent responsive web design, and you should look at them as models. But, there are many more, and I urge you to take some time and do a little research. By checking out what's out there and what others are doing on a core digital marketing element and you may get ideas for your site.

Domains and Web Hosting

The first thing to do is to register your domain name. Most nonprofits in the United States use an extension of .ORG or .NET. Nonprofits are not required to use these extensions, and some choose to use .COM, as most businesses do. Recently, other extensions were added to the list, and they are particularly helpful to nonprofits that work internationally. These new extensions are .NGO or .ONG.

Register your domain site as soon and as early as you can, while it's still available. You can register your domain with WordPress.org, Go-Daddy and other reputable companies for as little as $18 per year or less. Make your URL as easy to remember as you can, because it will inevitably become part of your brand. One of the things I do with my businesses is to pick up multiple URL domain names and extensions to protect my portfolio brands.

So, for example, my main website is found at WayneElsey.com. But, if you check out WayneElsey.net and WayneElsey.org, you'll see landing pages that I created. This helps to keep my brand identity consistent and protected. For me, it also helps direct customers for my various businesses into the proper websites.

When you select a domain name and provider, you'll also need to have a web host company. A web host simply provides storage space and access to your website. There are many competitive web hosts. I will make mention of one web host provider that provides qualified nonprofits with free web hosting, and that is Dreamhost[1].

Think About Your Website Plan

The next thing I do with my team when I'm developing a full site is to plan. We ask ourselves the elements that we want our website to encompass. Going back to my example, on the WayneElsey.com website, you're going to see a website that has an "About" page. It refers to the brands (with links so someone can easily navigate to any specific site they are interested in for more information). Additionally, you'll see news and media, my brand "Shop" and how to contact me.

If you were to check out the sites for .NET or .ORG, you'll find landing pages with a bit of the work we do and then the links to my portfolio brands.

When you are creating your websites and landing pages, you need to ask yourself what you want the people who visit to take away from it. Do you want them to learn about your organization? Do you want them to give (hope so!) or, perhaps, shop in your e-commerce store? Do you have

---

[1] Dreamhost Nonprofit Discount: http://wiki.dreamhost.com/Non-profit_Discount

events and want them to register on your website?

If you want your site to accept event registrations and donations (aside from using PayPal), you can check if your donation processing service (e.g. Network for Good) or constituent relationship management (CRM) provider (e.g. SalesForce Foundation). They may offer ways to set up your websites. Something that you want to keep in mind is that you want as much as possible to integrate technology to export easily information to help you review and analyze data.

Will you be incorporating a value-added blog into your website or have that as a stand alone? My nonprofit and social enterprise blog is a stand-alone website at NotYourFathersCharity.com. However, if you were to look through all of my websites, you'll find links that would direct you, easily, right back to the blog.

The Mystery of Search Engine Optimization (SEO)

Search engine optimization, or SEO, is not a great mystery. All it means is that you want to do everything within your control to make sure your website ranks at the top of search engines such as Google, Bing and Yahoo. However, this is an ever-evolving process as the search engines improve their algorithms and marketing pros become more expert at leveraging SEO to their advantage. So, the rules that may have applied only a few years ago, or even last year, may not apply today.

Keep that in mind. You want to make sure you're always staying ahead of the SEO game. As SEO becomes more advanced, you want to be mindful of certain things that will likely be core of good SEO practices down the line.

The first thing you need to remember and the thing that still rules is content. Your priority with SEO is remembering the adage that "content is king". You need to produce high-quality content, so your supporters and the public find you. The vast majority of online search happens on Google. Google has moved away from keywords toward content.

For instance, let's say you run a cancer support group. In the past, if you saturated your site with words associated with cancer and support, you were able to drive your website higher in the rankings. This is no longer the case.

Google has changed its algorithms, and it's now increasingly focusing on high-quality content. Now, you want to produce content in varying forms that play into the keywords. In other words, in the past, only the keywords mattered. Today, quality and varied content coupled with the keywords (now a secondary focus) is what increases your results in search rankings.

SEO rules require that content be written first for humans, with search engines as a secondary consideration. Search engines have become very adept at being able to discern between good and bad content. So, if you stuff your website, blog and articles with loads of keywords that are of low quality with poor grammar and phrases, you're running the risk of using a "Black Hat" SEO technique. There are other techniques spammers use to try to trick the search engines and find loopholes to get their websites higher in the rankings. This is not something you should be doing because you seriously run the risk of getting caught and blacklisted.

So, by remembering the simple rule that you are always writing high-quality content for humans and keywords is a secondary consideration, you'll be safe with "White Hat" SEO strategies.

The second thing you will want to work toward getting your website high in the rankings is to make sure that your website is indexed by the search engines. It's very easy to do this and if you search, for instance, "How to get indexed by Google", you'll find easy instructions.

What does indexing mean?

Again, it's very simple. The search engines use digital "spiders" or "bots" to "crawl" the Internet. When each search engine properly indexes your site and someone does a search for your organization or keywords, the search engine looks into its enormous directory. It then returns the most relevant results. Every time you change your website or add new content the search engines continue to update its indexing. This helps your search rankings.

A few other digital marketing strategies that you'll want to keep in mind for optimizing your SEO are as follows:

- Search engines, as well as social media platforms, are moving toward visuals. This is yet another reason to make sure your high-quality copy is accompanied by excellent visuals.

- Mobile, mobile, mobile! Need I say more?

- Make sure your content is shareable. Search engines are moving toward shareable content for higher rankings. If you're blogging or have key pages on your website you want shared, make sure you have the mechanisms in place. Provide your supporters easy and seamless share functionality of your content to their own followers on various social media platforms. In other words, have share buttons on your web pages and don't just rely on people to share a page URL. Make it seamless and easy!

• Online security is becoming increasingly more important, and it could affect your rankings. Make sure your website is using excellent security measures, especially if you are collecting sensitive end-user information. For example, make sure your website is using Hyper Text Transfer Protocol Secure (HTTPS), which is the secure version of HTTP. This is the protocol that handles data between the end user's browser and your website.

• Look at your conversion rates. It's pointless to be high in the rankings if people are not converting. Make sure you're seeing a positive ratio of people converting to take action because of what they see on your site. Conversion can be anything: becoming supporters of your organization, taking a survey, signing up for a newsletter or purchasing something from your e-commerce store.

Website Navigation Tips

When you're in the process of planning your website, one of the most important issues (besides being mobile ready) to consider is navigation. If people land on your site and they find it even remotely cumbersome, you've wasted your time and probably your money. I can't stress this enough: you want to make it easy!

When you're laying out and mapping your site, you want to think about primary navigation and secondary navigation. The difference is very easy to understand. Primary navigation is all the content that your donors and supporters want to find easily. This is the most pertinent information people will want to know about you. This will at least include your "About Us", mission, stories, and facts about your organization and donation pages. It can include a blog, membership or volunteer information.

Secondary navigation is information that you give people who visit your site, which is of lesser interest. This can be resources, news and media pages, your e-commerce store and your social media buttons.

As you're planning and designing your site, think about what is most important to your supporters and donors. Make sure you feature it as primary navigation content. In other words, make it easy to find.

Don't use words that people are not going to understand. You want the navigation bar and page titles to be easy and logical to follow–for just about everyone! Group content, if necessary and use drop-down menus from the navigation bar. For example, let's say your organization has various ways to get people involved. Perhaps you can have a group entitled "Get Involved" with a drop-down list of the ways to participate: volunteer, membership, donate, events, etc.

Your Available Resources

Once you've figured out what you want your website to do and how you want to engage your constituents and the public, you need to think about your resources. I'm mindful in writing this book that many organizations do not have a lot of money to spend. A real possibility exists that you're more than likely going to rely on your nonprofit staff to execute the creation and development of a new website. And, if that's the case, you may very well have individuals working on the project who are not designers and website developers. That's okay. Website development platforms today are easy to use and many cater to organizations and businesses that have a limited budget and do not know how to code.

With the tools that are available today, for instance on WordPress.org, it's free or inexpensive to have someone spend the time to create a basic website. Yes, you can also use WordPress.com and essentially create a site easily and for free, but you'll have your name with a "wordpress.com" extension. It's worth the few bucks a year to have your custom URL. WordPress has easy to use design templates and widgets, which enable you to capture information and embed pictures and, perhaps, videos.

However, if your team does not have some basic knowledge, the time, or you want to develop a robust and large site, it's easier to get an experienced volunteer. If you engage with a volunteer or low-cost website developer, just make sure you've vetted their work and obtained references.

And, don't forget, when the website is completed, you're going to need someone to maintain it! You want to make sure your primary website always stays fresh. It's also well worth it to get someone on your team trained in maintaining and updating your website(s).

Platforms for Developing Your Website

When you have moved on to actually developing your website, remember that you want the tool you use to be as easy and cost-effective as possible. There's no sin in that! Since you'll have to have someone on your team keeping your website fresh and a place where people will keep on coming back to see what's new, you want to choose a tool that will be easy to maintain.

There are a host of companies today that make it very easy to build a website on their platform. Check out some of the following companies: Squarespace, Wix, Weebly, and GoDaddy. I will tell you that I have some of my sites built on Wordpress.org. Although we have web developers, designers and experts who make our sites and those of our clients more robust, my team has found WordPress.org to be one of the easiest website building tools. If you or someone who is working with you knows it, there is no need to make a switch.

If you're looking to create your own mobile-ready website or easily maintain it, you'll find that WordPress is one of the easiest website and blogging platforms to use. And, that's what you want, whether or not you choose it. There's no need to invest thousands of dollars and loads of time trying to figure it out, especially if you're not trained as a developer or programmer. When you want to update copy, post pictures and videos, move pages around, WordPress allows you to do it easily. The New York Times and charity:water use WordPress. You may not be as large as those two organizations, but what that shows is that when you begin to scale-up, WordPress is flexible enough to allow you to grow.

Best Practices for a Website

So, how can you create a website that will be engaging and have people return?

- End-User - your website is about your end-user. That's the first thing you have to remember and keep in mind always as you are developing the site. You want to create a visually appealing website that provides visitors with the information they want to view. Good web design always puts the end-user first. Make sure every page makes sense and everything "fits" together logically.

- Google Analytics - it's important to have data. As you are building your site, make sure that your team uses Google Analytics or another analytics tool. Google Analytics is an easy to use reporting tool. It informs you about how many people have visited your website, what pages have been the most viewed, where people who are viewing your website come from geographically and more. If you're working with a developer and he or she decides not to use Google Analytics, make sure whatever tool used is easy and robust.

- Easy To View - You've probably heard about an "elevator pitch". You need to capture someone's attention in the amount of time, seconds, that it takes to get from one floor to another. This can translate to websites as well. Your site should be easy on the eyes. Use an appealing color palette. Use Sans Serif fonts, such as Arial. These are contemporary fonts that are easily read. The font size should be 16 pt. And, remember, pictures are worth a thousand words. If you go back to my earlier Nature Conservancy and Heifer International, you'll see a lot of pictures and graphics and limited text.

- Keep It Current - If your website has events that are now in the past, you need to update your site. As I've stated recently, I've seen plenty of nonprofit websites with events or pictures that took place months, if not years ago!

- Engagement - You want to have people coming back to your site. Give them reasons to come back. In your newsletters or updates, when people sign up for them, always offer plenty of links back to your site. Create a blog that is updated with fresh stories and interests on a weekly basis. Develop new and interesting podcasts. Remember, you're the expert!

- Navigation - You don't want people to get lost in your site. When you map it out, make sure that all links, pages and groupings make logical sense. Also, a rule of thumb is that it should not take a person more than three clicks to get to any page on your site.

- Link Rot - Test your links regularly. Link rot can happen without you ever noticing, and it tends to happen with older links. So, it's important to audit your website regularly and check to see that links are not broken. This is when you go to a page and your end-user sees an error message instead of what was intended. Your point person for website maintenance can check this out with an HTML validator and link checker.

• Call to Action - Ask. As those who visit your website scroll through any page, you should be looking to have them take some form of action. There are multiple ways to do this, including, donate buttons, surveys, buttons for social media, "Tell A Friend" or email capture widgets. There is an adage in fundraising; people don't give because they were not asked. Don't expect them to support you if you don't ask. Provide them with multiple ways to have them engage with your organization beyond the donation.

• Load Time - Individuals who visit your site are going to expect a website that downloads very fast, in 4 seconds or less. To help you do that with a simple site, make certain that your images are optimized with whatever platform you're using. Coding can also help. Have your website point person make sure the load time for the website is acceptable depending on the builder.

• Responsive Design - Mobile, mobile, mobile! I've said it before, but it's important to repeat, your website must be mobile ready in today's world. It needs to be a responsive design site. Your visitors are viewing your website from their computers, cells or tablets. Your site needs to look good on any of these devices.

Remember that your website is an extension of your brand. It's your calling card and the place on the Internet where you're establishing your formal presence. And, finally, if you're feeling daring and want to really get into ensuring your site is high in the rankings and converting visitors to become supporters, check out this free SEO starter guide from Google[2].

---

[2]http://static.googleusercontent.com/media/www.google.com/en/us/webmasters/docs/search-engine-optimization-starter-guide.pdf

FIVE

Aligning Your Social Media

"Build it, and they will come" only works in the movies. Social Media is a "build it, nurture it, engage them and they may come and stay." – Seth Godin

Social media is a big topic. It's one you'll need to master to be effective in today's world as it relates to engaging with your supporters and doing effective digital marketing. To understand social media, you need to know about social networking.

Social networking is one of the primary methods of communication in modern times. Because of technology, websites and applications (apps), we're now able to engage and interact with others who have similar interests anywhere in the world in real-time. Social media are the actual websites and app tools that we use to share content interesting or relevant to us in our social networking.

Here are some important facts about social media and social networking:

- 74 percent of users who use the Internet, engage in social media use.

- Fifty-five percent of those who engage with nonprofits via social media have been inspired to take further action.

- The majority of organizations say that their websites and email are the most important communication tools they use. Facebook is used by 97 percent of nonprofits.

- In case you're interested, here's a Wikipedia listing[3] of all the social networking sites that currently exist. As you'll see, there are a lot more than you think.

- Social media platforms are an ever-changing number, and who knows, maybe tomorrow the next Facebook can emerge. The most popular social media sites (full list) at present are as follows based on market share:

o Facebook - 53.4 percent
o YouTube - 17.2 percent
o Google+ - 4.06 percent
o Twitter - 3.1 percent
o LinkedIn - 1.78 percent
o Pinterest -1.4 percent
o Instagram - 1.3 percent

So, by looking at the above list, and with limited resources and time, where would you focus? Here's where we focus: Facebook, YouTube, Google+, Twitter, LinkedIn, Pinterest and Instagram. I will be frank that my businesses are more aggressive on some social media platforms than others, but we have a presence on all of them.

At the absolute minimum, you need to have an account on Facebook. But, you shouldn't limit yourself only to that social media tool. You should try to engage with your followers and supporters across various platforms because it increases the chances you'll reach more people. And, don't forget what you post on YouTube, for instance, you can share on Facebook and Twitter or Instagram for greatest exposure and impact. These companies make it simple to cross promote on their platforms. Of-

---

[3]http://en.wikipedia.org/wiki/List_of_social_networking_websites

ten, you need only press one or two buttons to have a post appear across multiple platforms.

As digital marketing continues to become more refined and advanced, investing your resources and time into social media will only help your organization. You'll gain more traction with followers and supporters.

How to Get Started Using Social Media

Nonprofits and social enterprises need to promote their organizations, get financial revenue, and raise brand awareness to fulfill their missions. Social media tools are a highly efficient strategy to do that, in a cost-effective way.

Keep in mind you have to look at social media beyond just tools to announce events or organizational activities. You need to become fully immersed in social media and think of it as more like a bridge to your supporters and followers.

If your organizational champions think and believe that you have built a secure and strong foundation for a bridge, they're going to cross it. If they see something that is done haphazard and with little value or thought to them, they're less likely to cross your social networking bridge. So you have to think of your followers and end-users first, just as you do with your website and other digital marketing elements.

What do your donors and supporters want to learn about what you do? What do they want to know about the field? This goes beyond promoting your activities. The most successful organizations (for-profit and nonprofit) in social networking are thought leaders in their respective fields. They consistently communicate information that is of interest to their followers.

To get started, it's very easy; just pick two or three social media platforms that you want to become expert in doing. That's really all you're going to need to do to begin. I would certainly pick Facebook as one of the social media tools I would use and post to it regularly (at least once daily). Facebook is very good for a variety of reasons: 1) you can post status updates; 2) you can easily post pictures and video (including those you post to Instagram or YouTube for increased engagement); and, 3) it has the largest market share of social media users by far.

What to Keep in Mind for Effective Social Networking

You'll want to build your followers on each of your social media platforms, which means you will have to be active on each social site you use. Make it a point to get on social media every day, and if you need to assign someone to the task, do it. Followers will stop following you if they are not seeing fresh content being shared by you or weeks between posts or tweets.

You want to have people follow you, but make it a point to follow others. Follow thought leaders in your field, associations, relevant publications and individuals who are aligned to your organizational mission and work. It doesn't matter where they're located. So, although most of your followers may be from your local area, with time, you may find that people are following–and supporting you–from clear across the world. Monitor who is following you and don't forget, to follow back!

I'm a big believer in humor and have written about it in the past. While humor has to be used smartly, it can communicate the lighter side of what you're doing and entertain. If a post is sufficiently entertaining, and perhaps humorous, it has the potential to go viral. This is what every business, nonprofit or social enterprise wants on the Internet. That's like the Holy Grail, but honestly, although having content go viral is great, it's not necessary to have a successful social media program.

Although it might be intimidating when you first start out on social media, you need to be responsive. I know that on some platforms, such as Twitter, it can seem like vast amounts of "stuff" is being thrown out there with no forethought. Smart marketers always know what they're putting out and why.

And then in happens. You get someone who likes a post, video or tweet. Or, someone takes the time to write a comment or send you a message. You need to respond, and you need to do it quickly. You want this engagement. Think about it as you would a telephone call, email or letter. In business, you want to respond quickly.

As always, you have to promote. Just because you have a Twitter username or Facebook page doesn't mean anyone is going to find it. You need to promote consistently offline and online. Sometimes, for instance, you will see my Twitter accounts asking followers to check out and follow our Instagram account. Make sure you have your social media platforms featured on your website and in all of your digital material or in whatever you do so people know where to find you.

Support others in your social media circle. Again, followers and the general social media universe are not interested in any brand that is simply promoting itself. People don't like to be sold to!

Put out articles or posts that help inform your followers–even when they are not written by anyone within your organization. If you see something that your supporters would be interested in knowing, even if it belongs to someone else, share it and give that person credit. This is good will that will benefit your organization in building its following. No one likes a self-promoting windbag. Period.

It is expected that you give your knowledge away as a value add. Yes, you need to give some of your expertise away. I do this on a regular basis, and it's something that the followers and supporters of my brands appreciate. Some of the things I have given away and promoted on social media, which took my team and me time and money to create, are as follows:

- A downloadable copy of my earlier book.

- All the promotional material for a shoe drive with my social enterprise, Funds2Orgs.com.

- Over 500 professional development resources for the nonprofit and social enterprise sectors at 501c3u.com.

Why do you want to give your knowledge away? Because it's value to your followers and the public at large. You want to show your supporters that you can give them, with high-quality content, what's of importance to them–for free. In return, you'll gain the loyalty of your followers and you'll gain new ones. Giving things away, in today's world, is simply smart business.

I'm not saying give everything away. We all need to make money, but be mindful that you're going to have to give some things away.

As often as possible, get in the habit of posting or tweeting your content using great photography and images. You probably have a personal Facebook account. Take a moment to scroll through your timeline. You'll notice by far that most posts and status updates are accompanied by visuals. There's a reason for this. Again, a picture is worth a thousand words. It grabs attention.

Finally, get messy. Don't be afraid to use social media as part of your digital marketing strategy and don't be afraid to make mistakes. There are no hard and fast rules about social media, but there are definite best practices. You'll start to see these practices in action the more your organization uses social media.

If you put out a tweet or a post that is incorrect, you can delete it. Yes, nothing is ever completely erased from the Internet, but if you're smart and engaging people in a positive way, you can do some of your learning on the fly.

Facebook and the End of the Free Ride

For many years, organizations that used Facebook as a key element of their digital marketing strategy were very happy. They're not so happy anymore. There was a time when nonprofits were able to create a Facebook page, place content on it and it reached many people who liked their pages. This is called "organic reach", in other words, posts that are seen by followers, which are not paid.

However, Facebook is a business, and it has to make a profit. This essentially means the free ride is over. Nonprofits that were seeing organic reach of 15 percent or more are now seeing 5 percent, or even 1 percent reach. Essentially, if you're not paying Facebook to boost your posts and have it reach your followers and beyond, it's going to take you a long time to get traction.

It's an easy question to ask: should I pay for boosting my post on Facebook?

My recommendation is you need to test it at the very least. Let's remember that Facebook is the largest social media platform in the world with over 1.23 billion accounts around the world. As it stands at the moment, there's nothing larger than Facebook, so it's something you need to consider.

As the importance of digital marketing grows Facebook is essential. If you have used Facebook, good for you, and remember that with the changed algorithms unless you're paying, the chances are that most of your followers will not be seeing your posts.

It's not expensive to test Facebook pages and individual posts. I understand that you may not have many financial resources, but you do have to make some investment to promote your brand. That's an absolute necessity. When looking to add social media into your overall digital marketing strategy, Facebook is an important element.

It can take as little as $5 to boost promotion on your pages or posts. And when you do, you'll suddenly find that your reach goes from perhaps a handful to hundreds or even thousands (targeted), depending on the size of your following.

When using Facebook, there are some things to keep in mind.

- Most people who like your page will never come back! To be effective on Facebook, you must have engaging posts. You need to give individuals a reason to come back to your Facebook page. Content is king. Period.

- In 2012, Facebook bought Instagram. As I mentioned earlier in this book, scroll through your Facebook timeline on your account. You'll see the majority of posts have visuals and video. There is a premium placed in social media to content that has visuals.

- When using Facebook, take a look and understand the data by using the Insights Analytics page. To be truly effective, you want to understand what's working and what isn't. Are some messages or posts performing better than others? That's what you need to know so you can engage and better target message to your audience. Facebook provides you information for your page–use it.

- Think about what happens when people visit your Facebook page. What action are they taking? Are they making a donation? Are they liking or commenting on your posts? Do you engage with them? You certainly want to have followers visit, but you also want them to take some action.

- Join groups on Facebook. There are plenty of organizations that are aligned with the nonprofit sector or your particular mission. Join them and engage with them on your social networking.

- Individuals on Facebook do not like to see "salesy" posts. No one ever wants to be sold to! If they see your posts crowding their feed with everything about your events and your fundraising, you'll soon not be on their feeds. You want to make sure you're posting several times a week. You want to place posts that they'll enjoy seeing–less on the self-promotion and more on the value you can provide your followers.

- Engage other organizations and follow their pages. Yes, this may sound counter-intuitive to promoting your social sector organization, but Facebook is about social networking. Look for social enterprises and nonprofits that are not directly competing with your organization and like their pages. This will increase your followers. Follow associations, your local chamber of business and others. Share their information and what you'll find is that when you share their posts, they'll share yours as well.

Feed the Beast of Twitter

Twitter is a whole other social media platform. It's very different from Facebook. Twitter is a micro-blog, and it's expected that organizations tweet much more often than they post on Facebook. Twitter is like a bottomless cauldron that needs to be fed continually. Thankfully, there are tools that help you "feed the beast" so you can be present to your followers without having to spend your entire day manually sending out tweets.

Although the majority of users are geographically located outside of the United States, we know that in today's world, the Internet has broken down borders. It is not unheard of to have supporters, followers and engage people on the other side of the planet. Here is what the Twitterverse looks like based on their own reporting:

- 288 million monthly active users
- 500 million Tweets are sent each day
- 80 percent of active users are on mobile
- Staff at the company also drink 585 gallons of coffee per week

(great fun fact)

To be present on a regular basis throughout the day on Twitter, automation is important. You'll want to use it to help you manage your followers and unfollowers. It'll also make it easier to help you tweet and engage your followers. Some tools for you to consider are as follows: Tweelow, Commun.it, @NonprofitOrgs and WeFollow.

When working on Twitter and automation of your tweets, what's important to remember is that you need to be thoughtful. It's not simply "set it and forget it". You have to think about the information you're putting out. What do your followers want to see from you? What types of tweets and hashtags? Your social media point person will have to be continually looking to see which tools are best for you and help you be the most effective.

If something is not working, then you have to make adjustments. Before we get to tips, let me tell you about some of the tools my team uses to automate the "drip" of tweets we send out across our accounts.

Bufferapp - helps you tweet and schedule content to your followers. Even on free accounts, you can schedule to upload to Twitter pictures and videos (as well as other platforms such as LinkedIn), which is important to draw attention to your tweets.

SocialOomph - this is an excellent tool for scheduling tweets, especially if you have multiple user account names. The free account, however, does limit you to Twitter (as opposed to having Facebook as well), and it does not let you upload pictures and video. That said, if you have multiple accounts, it's an excellent tool to use to schedule tweets. You can also manage every time another Twitter account mentions or retweets your tweet. This can help you engage with your followers and others by thanking them and responding to them.

Klout - Klout, as well as Bufferapp, suggests content based on keywords that might be of interest for you to tweet to followers. Also, with a free account, Klout does let you upload videos and photos. Klout also provides a Klout Score, which is a number between 1 and 100. The higher your number, the greater the influence you have on social media.

Hootsuite - Allows you to schedule tweets with videos and images. Within your dashboard, it can handle multiple Twitter accounts on one login account. It provides you a very good view of mentions and retweets so you can respond. If you go with the professional version, you can add Facebook and LinkedIn. You can also do good reporting and analysis with Google Analytics.

Here are some quick tips to help you be successful on Twitter:

1. Revisit your profile every so often. Update and refine it and make sure you add your organization's website URL.

2. Tweets under 100 characters have a higher engagement rate.

3. Use #hashtags. A hashtag is simply a word or very brief phrase

that groups all tweets with that particular hashtag together. So, for example, popular hashtags for nonprofits or social enterprises to use are as follows: #nonprofits, #philanthropy, #fundraising, #socialenterprise and #charity. You can also do a search on a regular basis of hashtags that you might be interested in and are trending.

4. Engage with others. Remember, this is all about social networking.

5. When you're referring to someone's article or find something of interest from someone else, mention the person or organization's Twitter username (@InsertName). You'll find that you will engage with others this way, and it'll also encourage others to retweet your content in reciprocity.

6. Use statistics and "Did you know" questions.

7. Use photos and videos. Users will find a 35 percent retweet bump if images are used.

8. Be consistent with the content you share. Every now and again, you may have a tweet on something not necessarily aligned to your work (perhaps inspirational quotes). However, the majority of your tweets should be around your mission, nonprofits, social enterprise, etc. Remember, you want to give your followers what they expect to see from you. It's probably incongruous to tweet out cooking recipes to your followers if you work helping save the whales.

9. As in Facebook, you can promote your tweets for greater exposure. Again, it is inexpensive and instead of having your tweets only appear on the timeline of your followers, it's a way to get your content to a wider targeted audience.

10. Always look for new followers, which means you need to follow and reciprocate on accounts that follow you.

Yes, You Need to Be On Google+

There's been a lot of talk about Google+ and whether organizations should have a presence on this platform. The answer is a resounding, "yes", for reasons you can probably guess. With Google driving the great majority of Internet searches, by default, Google+ is important. Most nonprofits have at least 50 percent of their search engine traffic come from Google.

Think of Google+ as a competitor to Facebook where you can post updates and content. Although Google+ is not as large as Facebook, again, Google is the largest search engine on the planet, by far. It's continually looking to integrate and index content so it's easily and seamlessly managed across all of Google's products (e.g. Google Calendar, Google Apps, Google Docs, Google Hangouts, etc.).

It's very simple. When you post to Facebook, make it a point to post on Google+, which can be automated. Just because it's Google, it means you need to be there.

The Visual Importance of YouTube and Instagram

Although I will not get too detailed into YouTube and Instagram, I do think that it's pertinent to write about them and their importance.

I've written about the need for excellent images and video that have to accompany the written content you're distributing. That's only going to grow more in the future. As a reminder, after Facebook, YouTube has the largest social media market share. Increasingly, now that videos are becoming an integral piece of other social media platforms such as Facebook and Twitter, nonprofits should not overlook YouTube. As you can see, the social media giants are playing off each other to make integration and the user experience as seamless as possible.

Nonprofits can create their YouTube channel so they can market and promote their brand within this particular platform and across other sites. Check out YouTube's Nonprofit Program, where they're assisting in developing your channel.

This particular program allows those who view your videos to donate to your cause right from YouTube; permits overlays for calls to action on your videos; provides access to production facilities in New York or Los Angeles; and, offers technical support. There are also guides so you can successfully promote your videos.

While I was working on writing this book, Instagram made a game-changing announcement. Instagram, similar to its parent company, needs to figure out how to make money. It announced that it was going to add Instagram buttons to posts, which rolled out as I was beginning to edit this book for publication.

Up until recently, when people saw something on Instagram that was of interest to them, they needed to snap a screen shot picture of it. If they remembered, they would then follow-up and research it on the Internet. A lot of the focus has been geared toward for-profit marketers who will now be able to integrate a shopping experience right from Instagram. But, it's important to know that this is also a boon for nonprofits and social enterprises.

The following buttons can be added to Instagram posts for, essentially, sponsored calls to actions (i.e. advertisements): "Shop Now", "Learn More", "Install Now", and "Sign Up". When I first read that Instagram had done this, before I saw the first picture, I was expecting some clunky ad functionality. I should have known better. The buttons below the pictures are truly seamless.

For nonprofits and social enterprise organizations, this means they can post fabulous pictures about their work, grow their following and test sponsored call to action buttons such as "Learn More" or "Sign Up". The opportunities are only limited by your imagination.

Social Media and Your SEO Rankings

Here's the deal. Social media tools are important for your search rankings. Again, you can have the most beautiful, mobile and easy to navigate website, but it takes more than that to keep your rankings on search engines high. Here's why:

- Being on social media, increases your presence on the Internet– organically, which boosts the likelihood that people will find you. You can then spend precious advertising dollars more strategically.

- Google uses Twitter to find new content to index. If your content is playing well on Twitter and being retweeted, this makes it easier for Google crawlers to find new content to index. That indexing is important for SEO because the more information you have indexed on Google, the better for your SEO.

- When a prospective donor or supporter is searching for your organization and brand, if you're on social media, this will help people find you easier within the search results.

- Your followers across various social media platforms will share, retweet or repost your content, which helps your exposure on search engines.

- The links people click related to your website and promoted through social media, helps boost your search rankings.

- Organic link building, whereby you put out content on social media that links back to your website or blog helps to drive engagement. Using strategic keywords on social media, your website and blog can help to increase your SEO efforts overall, again, boosting you on the rankings.

- In today's world, people will search for you not only on the Internet but also on social media platforms. You want to make sure you're present where people will be searching for you.

Periscope for Live Video Engagement

I've written about the importance of video and images across social media. Make no mistake about it, it's critically important. An additional social networking tool that I would like to mention that is a terrific resource for nonprofits to consider is Periscope.

This is a platform for live stream video. You will find articles that are hailing this social media tool as "revolutionary". The most important thing you need to know about Periscope is that Twitter developed it, which means Periscope plugs right into your existing Twitter followers. That is indeed revolutionary. You don't need to build another follower community.

But, there's more to the revolution. When you begin to film a live streaming event, it's available to anyone on your Twitter stream. What's more is that people can interact with you live. They can ask questions in real-time or share comments. None of this had been done before in one package.

So, how can you use it? Imagine any event that your organization is executing and think of a live stream to your virtual supporters and others. Let's say you have a walk, jog or race event, Periscope can be used to relay all the visuals and your information live. Additionally, supporters who are unable to attend can still attend remotely and share or comment on the event itself. They can ask you questions–and so can anyone else. This makes it an extraordinarily powerful tool to engage with your followers and the broader social media community at large.

There is no end to what can be live streamed: adopt-a-dog/cat events for greater exposure; a keynote address on a particular subject by your CEO; days of service from corporate funders who partner with you, etc. Really, you can let your imagination go here and live stream anything that will engage and help you promote your brand.

There is no better way that has been developed to date to stream an event live to your supporters, as well as the rest of the world. We've started to use it, and I'm very impressed. A member of my team has been "scoping" twice a week and engaging with professionals in the social sector. She always has a topic that she wants to discuss. She's relatable, and she engages with people who join.

That's the bottom line about Periscope.

I encourage you to check it out!

One final tool that some of my team members like to use for social media and general productivity automation on their mobiles is IFTTT. It's a great logic app. Essentially you create "recipes", which are based on "if/then" statements. More accurately: "If that, then that." The app gives you all the tools you need to create your own recipes or use many recipes that have already been developed.

So, for instance, you can create a recipe that if you have a new follower on Twitter then a welcome tweet is sent out automatically. Or, if you post something on Facebook then it also posts on LinkedIn. It's worth checking out and will help you automate not only social media, but also many aspects of your life!

SIX

Gain More Followers and Money

"People don't buy what you do, they buy why you do it." – Simon Sinek

You want your overall digital marketing efforts to give you more support-ers, donors and activists. So, as I was planning and writing this book, I wanted to speak to varying ways your organization can raise funds and get new followers.

With regard to online brand awareness and fundraising, there are definite strategies organizations should consider as they look to comple-ment their offline marketing efforts.

We've spoken about your website and how to improve it with your donate buttons, calls to action and the importance of mobile and images. Before we get to areas such as crowdfunding, there are still a few more things you can do on your website to help increase your revenue.

- Create ads for your appeals on your blog pages. Remember, you want to make it easy for people to give. If there's an ad with a com-pelling image and a call to action to donate next to what individuals are reading on your blog, it can help you raise more money.

- Provide your supporters and donors with various ways to get involved. Don't just have a donate button. Remember, to increase revenue, you also want people to get to know you. Add a web page that gives people who visit with "Ways To Support Us", and these can include volunteering and being social media ambassadors. You can also include ways to contribute with gifts of stock, planned gifts, matching gifts, in memory of and honor giving, etc.

• Make sure your donation page is geared toward sustainer giving. In other words, what you want to encourage individuals to give smaller monthly gifts (i.e. sustained) instead of donating a one-time gift. It is a known fact that supporters who contribute on a monthly basis give more than one-time donors. In fact, they give 42 percent more than one-time givers. A colleague of mine calls this "pizza giving". For the price of a monthly pizza, someone is supporting your organization.

• I know this one may sound obvious, but you'd be surprised by how many organizations don't yet publish an electronic newsletter, and if they do, it's very intermittent. If you want to increase brand awareness and fundraising revenue, you have to stay front and center with your donors and prospects. One way is to publish a newsletter that you email once a month. Make certain you have great photographs, give updates, always tell a wonderful donor story or two and always have links to pages on your site.

Email Outreach

I don't want to continue further in this book without talking about email fundraising. This is an important piece of the digital marketing and fundraising mix for social organizations. However, I realized in speaking with many directors of development that they made a decision not to write and send email fundraising letters.

Why? Many directors of development feel that email fundraising letters are too "salesy". They believe their donors don't want to receive them, and so they don't send them. But, this is a big loss of opportunity and revenue. It's also a lost opportunity to tell your story and perhaps have it shared by your donors.

A well-written and compelling letter, especially during the holiday season can bring fundraising dollars into your organization. It engages your prospects and donors. Additionally, people do share emails if they feel it's a cause that would be something another friend or family member would support.

Here's a fun fact, one-third of all fundraising dollars to nonprofits come in the last month of the calendar year. Email is a key part of your digital marketing and fundraising strategy, especially around the fourth quarter of the year.

Let's talk about spamming for a moment. If you have a list of emails with people who have no relationship to you and have never requested information or donated to you, you would be spamming if you send them anything via email. You do not want to engage in spamming.

Just so you know, if you spam, the following can happen to you if those who receive your email complain:

- Your Internet service provider and web hosting companies, who do not like working with businesses and organizations that spam, can close your account.
- You can get sued.
- Even if you have an "unsubscribe" link in your email, which you should always have regardless, if you continue to send them emails, you can be fined.

So, those are the spamming highlights. Quite simply, don't do it.

Instead, grow your database organically. It's important to offer plenty of opportunities for donors to register for updates or donate on your website. What you're looking for is to have them consent to be in your database. Your privacy policies, which should be easy to find on your website should include your policy about what you do with names and emails on your database.

I'm a big believer that if someone has been kind enough to register and join your database that their contact information should not be sold to third parties for list building. I won't get into that topic in this book beyond that point. But, be mindful that privacy is an important issue and supporters don't generally appreciate their private information being shared. If, however, you do buy lists and sell names and contact information, make sure that's clearly stated in your privacy policy.

Besides obtaining email addresses online, you also want to get them offline. You can do this when people are attending an event, but make sure they know that they're joining your database. When someone gives you their email address, it becomes a legitimate way for you to send emails (again, always having an unsubscribe link at the footer of the emails you send for your campaign).

Automate the process of acknowledgments. When someone signs up for your newsletter, donates, or registers their name on your website for updates, make it a point to send an automated acknowledgment. This will remind and confirm they registered with you.

Enhancing the Chances Your Emails Will Get Opened

I've spoken about mobile, and it's incredibly important to make sure every aspect of your digital marketing is mobile ready. That includes emails sent to supporters as part of your email fundraising campaign. Just so you know, according to one of the largest email campaign providers out there, Constant Contact, 66 percent of emails are now opened on mobile devices. Additionally, 80 percent of emails that can't be read properly on a mobile device are deleted.

A good email marketing and fundraising program should consist of the following:

- An engaging overall theme.

- A moving story or stories and engaging copy.

- Your email should be rich with visual images and graphics. Remember, it is very common for people to receive hundreds of emails in a day. They'll only spend a few seconds scanning it to see if they want to do anything or toss it. Images grab attention without words. If pictures or graphics get their attention, they'll spend more time and read.

- Short emails–somewhere between 400 and 500 words, including the call to action. This is not direct mail. We know that many non-profits in the past experienced great success with direct mail letters that were 3 and even 5 pages long. That does not work in email marketing.

- A schedule for your emails, goals and calls to action for each of your emails during a particular campaign.

- Send emails on Tuesdays, Wednesdays or Thursdays.

- Segment your list! Not everyone is going to respond to the same messaging. For example, you'll want to approach those who've never donated but have joined your database differently than you do regular supporters. One size doesn't fit all! Remember, it's always about people and what they want to see.

- Personalize emails. Avoid "Dear Friend" or "Dear Supporter". Use their name. Recognize their earlier gifts or actions using segmentation. People appreciate knowing what they've done for you.

- Subject lines that have a greater chance of being opened have between 50 and 60 characters in total.

- People scan their inbox very quickly before deciding whether to open emails. Use your organization's name in the "From" line. Don't use the name of a marketer or fundraiser most people wouldn't recognize.

- When your email is read, assume that only the top 25 percent to third will be read. So keep your focus and key messages at the top.

- Don't simply send out one email for your campaign. Appeals that have a series of emails (typically three) have the most success. Make sure in each email you include a call to action, whether it's to make a gift, forward to a friend or register for your activist campaign.

- Finally, you want to see performance and A/B test your campaigns and messaging. With respect to emails, you'll want to see the following:

o A good open rate for nonprofits is between 20 and 25 percent.
o Nonprofits should expect to see a response rate of 15 percent for their email campaigns.
o You should want to see a click-through rate (CTR) of about 3 percent. Your CTR means the click rate for links within the body of your emails.

o You'll always have attrition of your database and get people who will opt-out or unsubscribe from your database during your email campaign. That rate should be between 1 and 2 percent.

Crowdfunding Statistics and Platforms

The Internet continues to offer new and varying ways to diversify your organization's income stream. I'm sure that you've probably heard about crowdfunding. But, if you haven't, all it means is raising, typically, small donations from a large group of people. While the idea of crowdfunding has been with us for some time, the Internet has changed the game and how it happens.

MobileCause has published some interesting statistics:
- On average, an individual donates $66 to a crowdfunding campaign. In an article I wrote in the past for my blog, I noted how this amount likely exceeds the average one-time donation gift for many nonprofits.
- Nonprofits will gain 62 percent new donors and 28 percent of these new givers will donate again.

As for how much nonprofits raise on average, different credible sources have published varying numbers. Based on my personal research and expertise in the sector, I think we're not too off the mark using the following numbers as guides to success. MobileCause states the average nonprofit raises $568 per crowdfunding campaign. A very good infographic created by Craig Newmark, also published by Nonprofit Tech for Good, which compliments the previous number closely by MobileCause notes that the average crowdfunding campaign, with teams, was $9,238. And, we know there are organizations that have raised $75,000 or $100,000 crowdfunding. When you think about it, crowdfunding may indeed be a good fundraising tool for some nonprofits or social enterprises. I think organizations that do team events, such as walks or runs, should consider crowdfunding.

Organizations looking to get started in crowdfunding should know that the best approach for this form of fundraising is for a specific project or program. Crowdfunding shouldn't be used to raise general operating support. If you're ready to explore this 21st Century way of fundraising, then some crowdfunding platforms are as follows:

- Kickstarter - This crowdfunding platform is "all or nothing" for fundraising. In other words, you have to meet your designated goal to receive any of the funds.

- Indiegogo - This solution is the largest crowdfunding site with 15 million people visiting it each month.

- Crowdrise – If you work at a nonprofit, this is the leading crowd-funding site for causes. Barron's has featured it as a "Top 25 Best Global Philanthropist".

- CauseVox – Small and medium-sized nonprofits may appreciate this site, which tries to cater to those types of organizations. They try to make it as easy as possible.

- Razoo - Over $100 million has been raised for over 14,000 social organizations through this crowdfunding site.

Crowdfunding Tips to Maximize Fundraising

If you're considering embarking on a crowdfunding campaign, you want to remember that it's not only about the money. Crowdfunding has a major benefit besides raising funds for your nonprofit or social enterprise. That is, it helps elevate your brand's awareness and reputation in the public.

When you begin a crowdfunding campaign, you want to relay a compelling story to your supporters and the broader public. Crowdfunding is all about the images, video and a spot-on narrative. This is an opportunity to gain a wider audience as your supporters promote and share your efforts. It allows potential champions who don't know you to learn about your work. It also helps educate people about who you are and the impact you're having in society. Remember, on average, organizations will experience a gain of 62 percent in new donors and 28 percent of those will donate again.

- When doing crowdfunding campaigns, don't incentivize prospective donors with premiums. Your gift is not why supporters give.

They would rather you spend the money on your program than send them gifts in acknowledgment. Instead, develop creative ways to thank them. This could be done with high-quality photography, such as a compelling image related to your work.

• Crowdfunding is micro-fundraising. Think of it as fundraising in smaller bites. The campaigns that succeed best are those, which are for special projects with a finite fundraising window.

• Crowdfunding needs to begin with your supporters. There's no way around that. If you're expecting a bunch of new people who have no relationship to you to jump on the bandwagon, it's not going to happen. However, new supporters will come on board once they see traction on your campaign. So, a good rule of thumb, once you begin, is to seek to raise the first 30 percent within the first 48 hours–from your existing donor base!

• Momentum is important when you're crowdfunding. Promote your campaign, share success as you meet milestones on your way to the goal and use everything at your disposal. That means you should cross-market across all of your digital marketing and broader marketing efforts (e.g. email, newsletters, social media, website, donor meetings, etc.).

• Storytelling is important in all of your marketing efforts, and that includes crowdfunding. Remember to give the facts of your impact, but just as importantly, you want to get people emotionally invested in your work. This happens by speaking poignantly about one or two people being served by your organization. How is his or her life better because of the work you're doing? This goes a long way to engage people in the good work you're doing.

How to Go Viral

In my opinion, the greatest viral campaign in the social sector was the ALS Ice Bucket Challenge from 2014. YouTube has over 2 million videos that were uploaded in relation to the campaign. Facebook had over 28 million people take part by uploading videos, liking or sharing them on its site. And, ALS was the big winner with over $100 million raised. This was more than 35 times what they raised during the same period the previous year.

The phenomenon was incredible as it took the world by storm. That was a case of lightning in a bottle.

Look, the reality is that something like that doesn't happen every day. It's almost a year since the summer of 2014 when all you saw was the #icebucketchallenge. Nothing like that has happened since at that scale.

Will it happen again for another nonprofit or social enterprise? Yes, I certainly think so.

In today's world with social networking, marketers in the for-profit and non-profit sectors would love it very much if their content would go viral. I've heard folks who think something is going to go viral only for it to fall flat. We really don't know what triggers something to go viral, but there are certain steps that organizations can take to increase their chances.

- Be positive - Leading marketing experts agree. Positive content has a better chance of going viral than negative content. That makes sense. All day long, we're inundated with negative content on the news. People want something good. They want something fun. Being positive was a key reason the Ice Bucket Challenge went viral.

- Easy to share - People need to find your content so they can share it. By default, this means you need to be on the social networking sites where your supporters can find you. A presence on Facebook, Twitter or YouTube will go a long way toward helping your content to be shared by supporters, if not have something go viral.

- Hit an emotional trigger - Content goes viral when it makes an emotional connection. It triggers people to share it because it has touched them and elicited an emotion. The Ice Bucket Challenge was done for charity, which was important, but it was also fun! People wanted to see and engage their friends in something that was quick and fun. Everyone was having a good time and laughing when they saw the next video being posted on their feed or timeline. It was viral!

- Simplicity - For your content to go viral, less is more. Period.

There can't be complications. Going back to the great example of the Ice Bucket Challenge, there was nothing complicated about it. Essentially you donated to ALS, or you threw ice water over your head (or in some instances, both). You then nominated three more people to take the challenge. The whole thing took less than 2 minutes. It wasn't complicated or hard to understand.

- Call to action - Finally, you want something done if your content goes viral. If we take a look at the Ice Bucket Challenge, there were several calls to action done with masterful simplicity. After being nominated, people had 24 hours to complete the challenge. They were called to either donate or post a video of them getting soaked with ice water. Countless people did both–that's how ALS ended up with over $100 million. Finally, you had to nominate three people to do the challenge. I have to say, it was genius.

I want to make it a point to say that while the Ice Bucket Challenge was incredible and unique when it was happening nonprofit content has gone viral before and since.

The nonprofit, WATERisLife, created a video and hashtag (#firstworldproblems) and it brought attention to the plight of the world's poor in need of water. If you take a look at one of their videos, you'll see how they artfully mixed humor into topics as serious as poverty and lack of water.

A Playing For Change video was seen nearly 76 million times. They're a nonprofit and movement inspired to connect the world through music. If you take a look at the "Stand By Me" video, it was incredibly simple, but it connected with millions around the world.

Finally, while it's nice to have your content go viral, it's not the end all and be all if it doesn't. And, it doesn't mean you are failing! Not at all!

What you need to focus on is continually putting out high-quality content that is engaging, positive and inspires followers and supporters to take action. If something happens to go viral, that's great, but it's not necessary for a highly effective digital marketing effort.

SEVEN

Digital Marketing Trends That Will Affect You

"Marketing's job is never done. It's about perpetual motion. We must continue to innovate every day." – Beth Comstock

I don't think it's ever quite been like this. This is the digital age, and it began as a fire that is now an inferno of digital information. Last night I was reading yet another article about how the tech giants in Silicon Valley are looking to make sure every person walking on the planet has access to mobile phones and technology. It's in their DNA. It not only makes sense from a business standpoint, but it makes sense from a social perspective because of the benefits mobile access provides.

I like taking out my crystal ball and taking a look at the trends.

Why is it important to understand trends in digital marketing? It's very simple.

You want to have a proactive posture. You don't want to go for the train when it's left the station without you. As I've said often, chaos is the new normal. When you realize there are predictive threads in this tsunami of change and innovation, you're better prepared to ride the wave.

Here's what I see happening that you should keep in mind:

Google is the Master, But Maybe Not Forever

There was a time when you had the tech leaders of Silicon Valley publicly pronouncing the end of privacy. Then you had Eric Snowden and the world learned about mass data collection and suddenly, privacy was not so passé anymore.

With the ongoing hacking by governments, criminals and others into government and businesses, and more and more of our personal and public lives going onto the cloud, people are concerned about their digital lives.

While Google is still the king, and it could be a very long while until a company can effectively compete with it, you do have others entering into the search space. DuckDuckGo is a search engine that bills itself as, "The search engine that doesn't track you." Although Google does the vast majority of searches on the web, 7 in 10, DuckDuckGo is growing.

So what does this mean for you?

What it means is that as privacy continues to be a concern to people, you could end up with more of your supporters using other search engines. In turn, as people turn to search engines such as DuckDuckGo, it means that not only is the National Security Agency unable to track search engine searches, but neither are savvy marketers. This means that advertising can't be spent to track users' movements on the Internet, which then allow them to target advertising.

My main point here is that as a small nonprofit or social enterprise, it probably makes sense, as I advocated in the book, to gear your digital marketing to perform to the Google universe. But, keep an eye on what's happening in technology. If there's a catastrophic data breach–not that any data breach isn't bad to begin with–things can change as more people go to alternatives when using the Internet.

I think there's going to be a growing tension between the power of technology and the need for privacy. It's a fine line, but it makes sense for all organizations to be aware of the concern about privacy.

Digital Marketing is for the Warrior

With so many new companies being established, and platforms created to help feed the beast that is the Internet, digital marketing is not for the faint of heart. It's an absolute necessity in today's world. But, it takes a lot of time and thought day in and day out.

For small organizations, as you begin to build and expand your digital marketing and social media presence, you'll find that eventually you'll need to have this done by someone on staff. You may be using a volunteer, and I do suggest that approach if you don't have the funds. Ultimately, it takes a lot of time and energy to think about what needs to be happening 24/7/365 for your organization.

You need at least one person thinking about what platforms make sense for you. You have to know where your followers are and continually be connecting the dots to effectively cross promote. You want to deliver that fire hose of high-quality information that your insatiable followers and supporters want and demand.

Dipping your toe in the water isn't going to cut it. You have to dive right in and, if you have to, learn on the fly. There's no alternative in today's digital world other than to learn to swim as you're doing it. Marketers need to consume vast amounts of information so they can develop the skill to synthesize it and then turn around and send supporters what they want to see.

The User Experience Will Rule

I hope I've accomplished something very important in this book, and if I didn't here it is: donor experience is critically important. P = People.

There was a time when for-profit businesses and nonprofits dictated what and when information was delivered to their customers or supporters. Those days are done. Long gone. So, please don't think you can do that today and have it be sustainable long-term.

To be successful with your champions and the public, you need to have it ingrained that one size does not fit all. The Internet has opened up the world. While your donor profile might have been consistently one way in the past, it's changing–even if it's evolving slowly. When you're dealing with digital marketing and the Internet, you're dealing with the world.

New platforms and technologies are being unveiled at lightning speed. In the time that I was in the process of outlining and then writing my second book this year, the following occurred:

- Instagram unveiled its call to action buttons.
- The CEO of Twitter resigned.
- Periscope launched and continued to build its game-changing platform base.
- Google changed its algorithms to emphasize mobile.
- Mobile and mobile Internet usage continued to grow very quickly.

- Twitter and Google announced their partnership.

What does this mean?

It means that as a nonprofit or social enterprise, you've got to go with the times. There's no escaping it. If you want to grow your organization and reach out to a new stream of supporters, you have to go digital. And, if you go digital, you have to remember to try continually to at least stay with the curve. You have to have a presence where your users are (e.g. relevant social media platforms, etc.). You need to deliver the content they want to see from you!

You Will Have Access to More Data

Funders are demanding more data and metrics. That's a fact. Technology is making it possible to quantify impact in a way that's not static and is on demand. As donors continue to ask nonprofits and social enterprises to dive deeper in data, these organizations will increasingly rely on the power of technology.

The other side of data is that which comes from donors, supporters and volunteers. As I've mentioned before, there's a tension (rightly so) between privacy, social networking and revenue. This is going to be an ongoing debate. I believe we have only begun to scratch the surface of the vast amounts of data and metrics that can be gathered. With time, technology will become much more advanced and targeted, providing opportunity and threats.

Although there are nonprofits that do sell their less revenue producing names and contact information to data brokers to do list building, I think there's certainly a turn toward more transparency. As I've mentioned, if you're selling names, best practice dictates you let those who join your database know. If, however, you're not selling names, let people know on website privacy policies.

I think there's going to be much more refined donor data that nonprofits will be able to obtain. This is based on the amount of meta-data that's now being gathered by companies. More and more of our collective information is on the cloud on multiple databases. Make no mistake, our digital lives do leave tracks for others to follow and learn about us.

Mobile Advertising is an Ever Growing Part of the Digital Mix

I'll say it again. The free ride is over. It was great while it lasted, but technology isn't only disrupting whole industries, but it's also big business. Thankfully, it doesn't have to cost a lot to test Facebook posts or sponsored ads on Twitter. The price to begin to target market sponsored pages, posts and ads are reasonably low. This means most nonprofits should be able to dabble in paid advertising.

Facebook is the world's largest social media platform in the world with over 1.23 billion users. Over 1 trillion pages are viewed on Facebook each month. That's simply mind-boggling when you think about it. And, because of its market share, it reaches approximately 51 percent of all Internet users. Just this single platform provides an opportunity for your organization to reach (in a targeted way) countless thousands of potential supporters that align to your mission–anywhere.

Content Creators Have a Place at the Table

Because of the bottomless cauldron that exists now on the Internet, everyone's competing all day long with everyone else to cut through the noise–even just a little. If the Internet were a child, at this point, it would be having a loud temper tantrum. Get used to it. The Internet requires your attention.

That means that if you're not already doing so, you have to ramp-up your digital marketing game. The only way to do this is to work with designated content creators (writers and visual designers) whose job is to help you churn out high-quality content each day. You want to provide your supporters and followers with great content related to topics that align with your work. You want to have your marketers share content from others who complement the work you're doing and promote them. Remember, it's all about social networking and reciprocity is important in social networking.

But, while all of that content is going out, you also need to remind your supporters about your thought leadership and work. That means offering content through emails, electronic newsletters, blogs, ebooks, etc.

My suggestion is that you not only make sure you have a designated marketer, but you have content creators who are constantly working with your marketers. And remember, no one likes the sales approach. So, you have always to be mindful of that and make sure your content is value added for your supporters and followers.

Get Ready for More Payment and Donation Options

The genie is out of the bottle. Cold hard cash is slowly becoming a thing of the past. Even credit cards are being challenged by today's technologies. Since Elon Musk, Peter Theil, Mark Levhchin, Yu Pan, Luke Nosek and Ken Howery developed PayPal, there's been a push to change commerce, as we know it.

Tech geniuses are looking for the world to move to virtual currency. This is going to have enormous implications for governments, businesses, banks, and people. In fact, it's already started, and it's not going to stop.

How donors give money and how you pay for things on the Internet will probably change with time. Of course, it all depends on how governments and their lobbyists regulate what's happening with the transfer of money. But, I think it's only a matter of time before virtual currency becomes mainstream.

If you look at your own life, there was a time when you probably paid for a lot of your goods and services at the store in cash or credit cards. Then the Internet came. If you're like many of us, you may have a PayPal account. Perhaps your credit cards are saved on the websites where you buy goods. Maybe you set up automatic payments from your bank accounts for monthly payments. Have you noticed that wallets are slimmer these days? There's a reason. Those big, fat wallets of the past belong to the 20th Century.

Today, we have digital wallets. Apple has Apple Pay with its touchless technology. Its mobile competitor, CurrentC, has its QR code. Both companies, and others, are looking to allow people to pay for things or donate using their technology. These platforms are using your current payment types to pay (e.g. existing credit cards, bank accounts, debit accounts), but even what currency means is changing.

Bitcoin is interesting. Bitcoin is a virtual currency that operates independent of any central bank. No banks are involved whatsoever. As you can imagine, there's debate by governments and financial institutions about Bitcoin, but merchants do accept it. And, in 2012, the Bitcoin Foundation was established to spread the word in the social sector. Some, nonprofits have started to accept Bitcoin donations.

I think we may very well see a day when donations are made through your website or social media tools in ways other than inputting credit or debit card information.

And Just When You Thought…Guess What?

Digital marketing takes work. And when you're done with that, it takes more work.

We spoke in this book about the changes to Google and Facebook's algorithms. Guess what? They're going to change again. And, just when you thought you've got it, they're going to change again.

Expect as these businesses, and others, evolve and continue to perfect their targeting, that you'll be seeing more news articles with "algorithms changed" in the title. Remember, these companies want to make money and get even more precise on their targeting to increase market share.

It's all about money.

EIGHT

Social Sector Resource Guide

"There is a huge need and a huge opportunity to get everyone in the world connected, to give everyone a voice and to help transform society for the future. The scale of the technology and infrastructure that must be built is unprecedented, and we believe this is the most important problem we can focus on." – Mark Zuckerberg

During the time I've written this book so much has changed in the digital world. I'm sure once this book is published more will have changed. That's the kind of world we live in, and personally, I wouldn't have it any other way.

There's a tremendous amount of creativity, innovation and, yes, disruption that's happening in society and business. These are fascinating and high energy times.

There's something that I like very much about social networking. By definition, it means engaging with people. It means helping support and promote each other.

To that end, as I come to the end of this book, I'd like to give you resources of companies, colleagues and resources that I think are worth your time to check out.

I hope this book's given you some insight on digital marketing and its varying threads. And, I hope the following resources will give you further benefit. We're all in this together. We want to make the world a better place.

- **Nonprofit Tech for Good:** It has over 100,000 monthly visitors. It also has more than one million followers on social media. Nonprofit Tech for Good is a leading social and mobile media resource for nonprofit professionals.

- **Beth's Blog:** Beth Kanter discusses social media and marketing for nonprofits on her blog. She is the co-author of The Networked Nonprofit.

- **National Council of Nonprofits:** Social sectors leaders and employees can find resources and content related to topics such as board governance, fundraising and leadership.

- **Skoll World Forum for Social Enterprise:** Social entrepreneurs can learn the latest news and innovative approaches in a variety of focus areas (e.g. education and economic opportunity, environment and healthcare).

- **Charity Navigator:** The most used charity evaluator in America.

- **Stanford Social Innovation Review:** SSIR is an award-winning magazine, blog and website that covers cross-sector solutions to global problems for nonprofits and social enterprise.

- **NTen: Nonprofit Technology Network:** NTEN aspires to a world where all nonprofit organizations use technology skillfully and confidently to meet community needs and fulfill their missions.

- **Pamela Grow:** this site is focused on helping one-person operations to develop and implement strategies to raise money and "grow".

- **Not Your Fathers Charity and 501c3U:** You didn't expect me to leave out my social sector blog and online university with hundreds of free resources, did you?

Best Nonprofit Apps Available on iTunes and/or Google Play

Check out these apps so you can see other examples of good mobile design.

- **SafeNight:** When someone is in urgent need of safe shelter to escape domestic violence.

- **Charity Miles:** Exists to help you change the world by earning corporate sponsorship for charity when you walk, run or bike.

- **iCitizen:** A free nonpartisan, civic-engagement platform that offers a unique way for you to reconnect with politics and government.

- **PETA:** Is PETA's mobile app to take part in urgent action against animal cruelty and to donate.

Best Marketing Resources for Social Sector Organizations

In addition to the resources I've given you in the book, here are some others:

- **#NPMC Chat:** Nonprofit MarCom Community created this Twitter hashtag. You can join their Twitter chats using #NPMC. However, to be more effective and focused, they recommend you join their chats with services such as tchat.io, twubs.com or TweetChat.

- **American Marketing Association Foundation:** This association gives social sector organizations marketing support for, which benefits society.

- **Social Media for Nonprofits:** This organization looks to promote social media for social good. They have conferences, a blog, online learning and Tweetchats.

- **About.com:** Experts in the social sector give information and advice for nonprofits and social enterprises. Just key into their search bar "marketing for nonprofits" to get results.

- **Nonprofit Marketing Guide:** This site gives one-person and small shops with tips and training for do-it-yourself marketing.